SETTING DOWN
THE RUCKSACK

A FIELD MANUAL FOR WINNING
THE WAR WITHIN

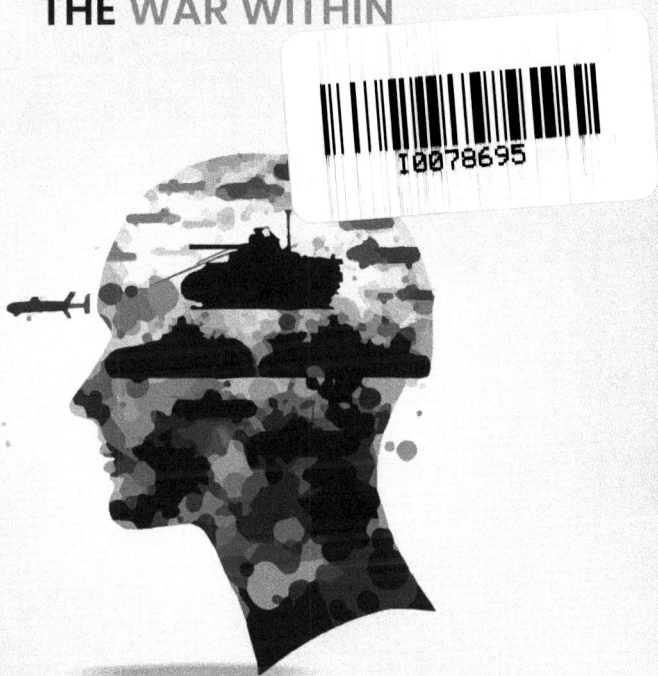

DEMETRIUS IRICK

DEDICATION

For the ones who served, the ones who returned, and especially for the ones who didn't.
And for the families who serve alongside them, holding the line at home.

This is for you.

Author's Note: My Mission to Our Community

Before we begin, I want you to know who you're hearing from. My name is Demetrius Irick. I'm a veteran of the US Army, serving from 1991-1998. I'm a certified life coach and a meditation teacher. But the most important thing for you to know is that I am a survivor.

There was a time after I came home from the service when I was a ticking time bomb. I was haunted by memories and crushed by the suffocating guilt of being alive when so many of my friends didn't make it.

I didn't know how to carry it. So, I tried to numb it. I drank a lot to drown the pain of all the unhealed trauma I experienced in my life. I engaged in risky behaviors, things that degraded the man I had fought to become. My life was spiraling out of control. After many arguments with my wife, it finally happened. I fell asleep at the wheel.

The DUI was one of my rock bottoms. The one that forced me to finally act.
That was the moment I knew I had to stop running. I had to turn and face the predator that was hunting me. I made a decision: I have to conquer this demon and begin the inner healing.
That path forward, for me, was a combination of therapy and the daily practice of meditation. It wasn't a magic pill. It was work. And it's still work. This ain't no "I have arrived book!" It was a practical, no-B.S. tool that allowed me to assess my own

inner turmoil and respond with a clear mind. It gave me a way to finally set down the rucksack of my past without discarding the lessons it taught me.

The impact on my own life was so profound that I knew I had found my new mission. I pursued certifications in life coaching and meditation instruction, dedicating myself to translating these practices for our community—stripping away the jargon and focusing on what works for a warrior's mindset.

This book is the culmination of that journey. It combines my lived experience as a veteran who hit rock bottom with my professional expertise as a teacher who found a way back. The techniques you'll find here are the very same ones I used to find my own footing.

This isn't just theory. It's field-tested on the most difficult battlefield of all: the one inside your own mind. My mission now is to get these tools into your hands. Welcome home.

TABLE OF CONTENTS

PART I: THE MISSION BRIEFING - GETTING STARTED

Chapter 1: Your New Orders

Mission Briefing - From a Professional Peer

Alright, let's talk, straight up. No B.S.

If you're reading this, you're part of the tribe. You've worn the uniform, or you've stood by someone who has. Like you, I know what it means to stand a post, to feel the weight of that rucksack dig into your shoulders, and to operate in places where being switched-on isn't just a state of mind—it's what keeps you alive.

But I also know what happens when you can't find the 'off' switch. For a long time, I was skeptical of anything like "meditation." It sounded too soft for the problems I was facing. But I was looking for a practical tool, not a new belief system. And I found one.

As a veteran who went on to become a certified meditation teacher and life coach, I've seen these tools work. I've used them to navigate my own darkness, and I've taught them to service members and veterans who are looking for a way to get a handle on the noise.

This book is a field guide. It's about mindfulness as a tactical skill. Think of it as PT for your brain or weapons maintenance for your focus. It's the practice of taking a "standstill"—a deliberate pause to assess, regroup, and act with clarity, not just instinct.

My goal here is to give you the tools that helped me find my own ground. They're designed to help you:

- Sharpen your focus when it matters most.
- Get a handle on your stress reactions instead of letting them run the show.
- Find your footing on the home front, whether you're newly transitioned or decades out.

The mission is simple: to engage with these practices. To give them the same seriousness you'd give any part of your training. This isn't about changing who you are. It's about reclaiming the best parts of the warrior within you—the strength, the discipline, the resilience—and bringing that warrior home, truly home.

Let's get to work.

Chapter 2: Why This Isn't B.S. - The Science of Mindfulness and Performance

I know what some of you might be thinking. "Mindfulness? Isn't that some soft, spiritual stuff?" I thought the same thing. I'm a practical person who needs tools that work, not theories that sound nice. So let's talk about what's actually happening in your body and your brain when you practice these drills. This isn't magic; it's physiology. Physiology is simply the way your body and its parts function.

To understand this, let's look at the chain of command inside your own head. Think of your brain as having two key players that mirror the military's own structure: the Enlisted soldier on the front line and the Officer in the command post.

The Guard in the Watchtower: Your Enlisted Force

Deep in your brain, you have a part called the amygdala. For our purposes, this is your Guard in the Watchtower—your front-line, enlisted soldier. This soldier is your first line of defense. They are powerful, fast, and react instantly to any perceived threat. They are the heart of the operation, the ones who get things done. There is no military without the enlisted soldiers, and your body can't survive without this Guard.

When this soldier spots danger, they hit the alarm, triggering your sympathetic nervous system, which you know as the "fight-or-flight" response. Your heart hammers, your vision narrows, your hands might shake, you stop hearing things clearly, and your ability to think rationally vanishes. It's what's behind explosive anger, crippling anxiety, and the impulse to either run or fight. This response is meant to save your life, but when it's triggered constantly, it degrades you.

The Commander in the HQ: Your Officer Corps

The other key player is your prefrontal cortex. This is your Commander in the HQ—your Officer. This is the part of your brain responsible for strategy, rational thought, complex problem-solving, and emotional regulation. Your Commander has the big picture, the training, and the experience to make smart, long-term decisions.

But here's the truth every enlisted soldier knows: the officers can't do their jobs without us. The Commander in the HQ is useless if they can't communicate with the soldier on the front line.

The Breakdown in the Chain of Command

Here is where the age-old battle plays out inside your own skull. When your Enlisted Guard gets overwhelmed by incoming fire—whether it's real danger, a painful memory, or the stress of a failing marriage back home—they get so loud and panicked that they stop listening to the radio. The Commander in the HQ is shouting orders, trying to implement a strategy, but the Guard can't hear them. They are acting on pure, raw instinct.

This is an "amygdala hijack." It's when your front-line soldier takes over the entire operation, and your smart, experienced

Commander is cut out of the loop. This is exactly what was happening when I was nose-to-nose with that drill sergeant. My Guard was in complete control, and my Commander was nowhere to be found. The breathing was my way of getting him back online. This is when you make bad decisions that can bring down your entire personal military.

Taking Back Command

The tools in this book are about restoring the proper chain of command. Practices like Box Breathing are how the entire system learns to function correctly under pressure. When you intentionally slow your breathing, you are the Commander in the HQ sending a direct, clear signal to your Enlisted Guard: "I hear you. I see the threat. Now stand down and follow my orders. I have a plan."

You are activating your parasympathetic nervous system—the "rest-and-digest" system—which tells your Guard that the immediate crisis has been assessed by command and it's time to get back to the mission plan.

Rewiring Your Unit

The most important part is that you can rewire this relationship. Your brain has neuroplasticity, which just means it can change. Every time you practice a mindfulness drill when things are calm, you are running comms checks between your Commander and your Guard. You are building trust and strengthening that connection. You are training your Guard to be less jumpy and to trust that the Commander has the big picture in mind.

You are building a more cohesive and effective internal military. This isn't about becoming less of a warrior. It's about ensuring your command structure works flawlessly, so the right part of you is in charge when everything is on the line.

Chapter 3: The Rules of Engagement - How to Use This Guide

Before we begin the hands-on portion of this guide, we need to establish the Rules of Engagement. How you approach this training will determine your success.

The single most important rule is this: Think of this as Mental PT.

Remember when you first got to Basic Training? Most of us didn't start out as physically fit soldiers. We couldn't run for miles or do endless push-ups. We got to peak performance through one thing: a daily, disciplined system. You were likely in the best shape of your life during or right after Basic. It wasn't because of one brutal workout; it was because of the relentless consistency of the system they established.

The same principle applies here. This is your new PT plan for your mind. To make it work, you will follow three simple rules of engagement.

Rule 1: Consistency Over Intensity.

Just like in the gym, five minutes of practice every single day is infinitely more effective than trying to do a marathon session once a week. Your mission is to create a new habit. Attach it to an existing one—do it for a few minutes right after you wake up, or right before you go to sleep. Make it part of your daily routine. The system is what builds the strength.

Rule 2: A Wandering Mind Is a Rep, Not a Failure.

This is the part where most people get frustrated and quit. Your mind will wander. That is what minds do. They think, they plan, they worry, they remember. Do not get angry at yourself for this.

Let's go back to the PT analogy. When you're lifting a weight, the goal is the muscle contraction—that single repetition. In Mental PT, the moment you realize your mind has wandered off-mission and you gently guide it back to your breath or your anchor—that is the rep.

The wandering isn't a failure. The act of returning your focus is the success. Each time you do it, you are strengthening your focus muscle. Acknowledge the thought, let it go, and return to the drill. One rep at a time.

Rule 3: Follow the Orders, Don't Chase Feelings.

Your job is not to "feel peaceful." Your job is not to "get calm" or "empty your mind." Your job is to follow the instructions of the drill.

Focus on the count of your breath. Focus on the physical sensation of your boots on the floor. Execute the steps as they are laid out. The results—the calm, the clarity, the focus—are a byproduct of the work. They come with time and consistency. If you go into a session trying to force a feeling, you will fail. Trust the process. Follow the orders and let the results take care of themselves.

That's it. Those are your rules. You are now ready to begin your training.

PART II: BASIC TRAINING - CORE SKILLS

Chapter 4: The Tactical Pause - Your Three-Second Reset

The pressure comes on fast. A sudden change in orders. A piece of gear malfunctions. A tense interaction with a superior. In these moments, the body's threat response system kicks into high gear—heart rate spikes, breathing gets shallow, and your focus narrows to a pinhole. This is the "fight or flight" instinct. It's great for immediate survival, but it's terrible for clear decision-making.

In the field, you can't afford to be reactive. You need to be responsive. A response is considered; a reaction is instinctual and often sloppy. The space between that initial trigger and your action is where a battle is won or lost. I learned the hard way that a reaction isn't the same as a response.

- ✓ Reactions got me in trouble.
- ✓ Responses are considered, they're clear.
- ✓ That space is the Tactical Pause.

Taking a tactical pause isn't about stopping. It's about taking a moment to gather intel on your own state so you can act with precision. You don't need a quiet room or a yoga mat. You can do this standing in formation, sitting in a Humvee, or before stepping into a difficult conversation. I started practicing this when the stakes were low, so the skill would be there when the stakes were high. It's a three-second drill that changed how I operate.

Drill: The Three-Second Reset

- **Mission Objective:** To create space between a trigger and reaction
- **Mission Time:** 3 Seconds
- **Recommended Frequency:** As needed in any moment of stress. Practice often when stakes are low to build the habit.

  - Anchor: Feel your feet on the ground. Whether you're in boots or shoes, notice the solidness beneath you. This is your anchor point. It's real, it's present.
  - Breathe: Take one deliberate, slow breath. In through the nose, feeling your chest or belly expand. Out through the mouth, controlled. Don't make a show of it. This is for you and you alone.
  - Assess: As you breathe, bring your awareness to one physical sensation. The feeling of the rifle sling on your shoulder. The steering wheel in your hands. The air on your skin. This pulls your focus out of the chaos in your head and into the physical reality of the moment.

That's it. Three seconds. Anchor, Breathe, Assess.
What you're doing is short-circuiting the panic signal. You are telling your body, "I am in control." You are creating just enough space to let your training, your intelligence, and your discipline take the lead, instead of your raw nerves. The tactical pause is your mental cover and concealment. Use it to gain the advantage.

Chapter 5: Box Breathing - Controlling Your Response Under Fire

Let me tell you about the first time I truly understood what it meant to control my response. It was day one of Basic Training at Fort Knox. I was fresh off the bus, and a pack of drill sergeants descended on us, a whirlwind of yelling, cursing, and spit.

One in particular, a rough, red-faced drill sergeant, got right in my space. He looked me up and down, his eyes narrowed. "Irick," he growled, "why you eyeballing me?"

Before I could even process the question, I was on the ground. "Don't get up until I tell you," he screamed. From that moment on, he was on me. Relentless. For weeks, he was my personal demon, riding me into the ground every single day.

I remember one time, we were nose-to-nose. He was screaming, just unloading on me, and bits of his chewing tobacco were hitting my face. The rage that boiled up inside me was white-hot. It was so absolute, so overwhelming, that in my mind, I had already crossed the line. I'd already punched him square in the face. I'd choked him unconscious. I had achieved total, glorious, and self-destructive victory.

My career would have been over. My life would have been irrevocably altered.

But as that mental movie played out, something else took over.

A deeper, quieter instinct. Without a name for it, without any formal training, I started breathing. It was slow. Intentional. A deliberate inhale, a pause, a controlled exhale, another pause. While my mind was a screaming chaos, my lungs were performing a calm, disciplined drill.

That slow, rhythmic breathing was the only thing that stood between me and total destruction. It created just enough space between the drill sergeant's screaming face and my reaction. It was the circuit breaker. It allowed me to take the rage, acknowledge it, and file it away instead of letting it run the show. I didn't win the fight in my mind. I won the real war—the one for control of myself.

I didn't know it then, but what I was doing was a raw, desperate version of a technique called Box Breathing. It's a tool used by everyone from elite special operators to emergency room surgeons to control the body's physiological response to extreme stress. When you're under fire—whether that fire is literal or a drill sergeant's spit—your sympathetic nervous system lights up. It's the "fight-or-flight" response. Box Breathing is the override switch. It manually takes control of your breathing, and in doing so, it sends a signal back to your brain: I am in command here. It's not about becoming passive. It's about becoming precise. It's how you respond, not react.

The Drill: How to Box Breathe

1. **Mission Objective:** To regain control of your nervous system during a high-stree event.
2. **Mission Time:** 1-2 Minutes (for three to four

repetitions)

3. **Recommended Frequency:** Daily to build the skill, and as needed to manage high-stress "fight-or-flight" responses.

- Inhale for a count of four. Slowly, through your nose.
- Hold for a count of four. Don't clamp down, just hold steady.
- Exhale for a count of four. Controlled, through your mouth or nose.
- Hold for a count of four. Hold the lungs empty.

That's one repetition. Do this three or four times. You are literally creating a box with your breath.

Warning Order: Avoid This Common Mistake

Let's address the false narrative right now. The biggest mistake you can make is having the misconception that this is supposed to make you holy, a saint, a yogi, or a monk. The goal isn't to find "instant peace" and float away. That's a myth.

So have no agenda when you do this.

Your mission is not to feel peaceful.
Your mission is simply to count to four, four times.
That's it.

Just focus on that moment—those few seconds of inner stillness required to complete the drill. Stay right there. Don't worry about what it's "doing." Just execute the maneuver.

Execution: How to Make This Work

Think of this like PT for your mind. You are building a muscle. You are building your inner peace. The first time you do a push-up, you don't expect to be able to do one hundred. It's the same here.

The key is consistent behavior. With time and practice—doing a few reps every day—your mind will begin to recognize the signal. It will learn that when you start this drill, it's time to begin a calming state. It will happen at the mere intent to meditate.

Your job is not to force peace. Your job is to create the habit. The rest will follow.

Chapter 6: Anchoring - Using Your Senses to Find Solid Ground

We were on a range, a live ammunition training. The air was electric with chaotic energy. The world was nothing but sound and vibration—the deafening crack of rifles, the sustained chatter of rapid fire, the hiss of tracer rounds cutting through the air.

For most people there, it was just another training day. For me, it was something else.

Before I joined the service, I lived a different life. I was in the streets, hustling, caught up in a world of drugs and violence. I've seen things—drive-bys, shootouts, murder. I'd had several near-death experiences that I was lucky to survive. And in the middle of that live-fire exercise, my past came rushing into my present.

The noise, the smell of cordite, the controlled violence—it all triggered something deep inside me. The stress, the panic, the anxiety—it hit me like a physical blow. I was paralyzed. I was there, in my gear, on the range, but I was also not there at all. It felt like I was watching a movie of myself from somewhere outside my own body. My throat seized up, like a golf ball was lodged in it. I couldn't speak. I couldn't move. I couldn't breathe.

I was completely adrift, lost in the storm of my own memories. And then, I saw it. In the midst of all that chaos, all that noise and rapid fire, there was a squirrel. Just a squirrel, off in the distance, doing what squirrels do. I don't know how or why my eyes locked onto it. But in that moment, everything else fell away. I zeroed in on it. I watched its tail flick. I saw it dig at the ground.

It was real. It was alive. And it wasn't part of the chaos. It was just... there. Watching that squirrel was a lifeline. It gave me a split second to return to my body. The golf ball in my throat loosened. I could feel the weapon in my hands again, feel my boots on the dirt. The movie ended, and I was back on the range, present and able to function.

That squirrel became my North Star. In land navigation, no matter how disoriented or lost you get, if you can find that one fixed point in the sky, you can reorient yourself. You can find your bearing. You know where you are and which way to go.

An anchor does the same thing for your mind. It's a fixed point in the present moment that you can latch onto to pull yourself out of the mental storm. When your mind is being hijacked by past trauma or future anxieties, an anchor is your way of planting your feet back in the here-and-now. As my story proves, it doesn't have to be profound. It can be a crack in the pavement, the feeling of a cold water bottle in your hand, or a squirrel on a firing range.

This is a skill you can practice. You don't have to wait for an anchor to randomly appear; you can create a drill for finding one.

The most effective method I teach is the 5-4-3-2-1

Grounding Technique. It's a systematic way to force your mind to engage with your senses and report back on the present moment.

The Drill: 5-4-3-2-1 Grounding

- **Mission Objective:** To pull your mind out of a mental storm and into the present moment.
- **Mission Time:** 1-2 Minutes
- **Recommended Frequency:** As needed when feeling overwhelmed, anxious, or disconnected from the present moment.

  - *ACKNOWLEDGE* five things you can **SEE**. Look around and name them silently to yourself. There is the rifle muzzle. There is the green grass. There is my teammate's helmet. There is a cloud. There is my left boot.
  - *ACKNOWLEDGE* four things you can **FEEL**. Bring your awareness to physical sensations. I feel the grip of my weapon. I feel my body armor on my shoulders. I feel a breeze on my neck. I feel my tongue on the roof of my mouth.
  - *ACKNOWLEDGE* three things you can **HEAR**. Listen past the main noise. I hear my own breathing. I hear the wind. I hear the distant sound of a vehicle.
  - *ACKNOWLEDGE* two things you can **SMELL**. This one can be subtle. I smell the gunpowder. I smell the dirt.

- ***ACKNOWLEDGE*** one thing you can **TASTE**. I can taste the salt from my sweat.

By the time you get to the end of this drill, you will be back in your body. You will be back in the present. You have taken command of your focus and anchored it in reality. You are on solid ground.

Chapter 7: Mindful Observation - Sharpening Your Situational Awareness

You know the tension of a barracks inspection. The air is still, thick with the smell of floor polish and the silent fear of the gig line. Everything is supposed to be perfect—a sterile, orderly world where every corner is a perfect ninety-degree angle and every surface gleams.

I remember standing at attention by my bunk, heart pounding. My bunk buddy, in a moment of sheer panic, had contraband: a pack of cigarettes. He thought he was clever, trying to hide it in a tiny crease he made in the crisp folds of his bed. To a quick glance, it was invisible. He had looked at it and thought it was hidden.

But we weren't dealing with a quick glance.

The drill sergeant entered the bay. He didn't just walk; he glided, his presence sucking all the air out of the room. He didn't just look; he scanned. His eyes moved with a slow, deliberate intensity, not just searching for dirt, but observing reality itself. He was seeing the world as it was, not as it was supposed to be.

He paused at my buddy's bunk. His eyes swept over the perfectly made bed once, then twice. He tilted his head slightly. Without breaking his stride, he reached out one hand, unfolded a single crease in the blanket, and plucked the cigarette pack out. He held it up, said nothing, and let the crushing silence do the teaching.

He found it in a split second. And in that split second, I was reminded of a fundamental lesson: the importance of paying attention to the details. My buddy looked; the drill sergeant saw.

That is the essence of Mindful Observation. It's the difference between the blank stare of a bored guard and the active scan of a seasoned warrior. It's the ability to see the world with fresh eyes, free from the filters of your own expectations, judgments, and mental noise. It's the core of true

Situational Awareness

The same keen eyes that find a hidden pack of cigarettes in a folded blanket are the same eyes that spot the subtle glint of light on a sniper scope. It's the same focused hearing that distinguishes the sound of a faulty engine from normal road noise. It's the same awareness that feels a subtle shift in the mood of a room before things go south.

This isn't a magical power. It's a muscle you train. You train it by practicing observation when the stakes are low, so the skill is there when the stakes are high.

The Drill: The Coin Study

- **Mission Objective:** To train your mind to stay on-target and see what is actually there.
- **Mission Time:** 2 Minutes
- **Recommended Frequency:** Once or twice a week to

deliberately sharpen your observational skills.

- Find a coin. Any coin will do.
- Set a timer for two minutes.
- Place the coin in front of you.
- Observe it. Your mission is to use these two minutes to see everything there is to see about this coin. Notice the scratches. The date. The way the light hits the raised edges. The specific texture of the metal. The tiny letters. The nicks and dents that make this coin unique.
- When your mind wanders (and it will), just guide it back. The thought "this is boring" is a distraction. The thought "what am I doing later?" is a distraction. Gently release them and return your full attention to the coin.

What you are doing is training your focus. You are teaching your mind to stay on-target, to see what is actually there, not what you think is there.

Connecting Your Internal and External SA

So, why does all the internal work we've done—the breathing, the grounding—matter for external observation? Because the drill sergeant could see that pack of cigarettes for one simple reason: his mind was clear.

He wasn't distracted by his own mental noise. He wasn't thinking about what he was having for dinner, or annoyed about a conversation he had that morning. He was fully present, his focus like a laser.

If your mind is a raging storm of anger, anxiety, or boredom, your ability to observe the outside world is compromised. You will miss things. Learning to notice your own internal state—to know "I am feeling agitated right now"—is the first step to setting it aside so you can see the world with clarity. A clear mind sees the truth.

PART III: FOR THE ACTIVE-DUTY WARRIOR - ON THE FRONT LINE

Chapter 8: Managing Pre-Deployment Stress and Uncertainty

The last few weeks are a blur of checklists, packing lists, and "hurry up and wait." It's a whirlwind of activity on the surface, but underneath it all runs a single, cold current: fear. The fear of the unknown.

And that current hits its peak in the final moments. The angst of goodbye.

You're standing there with your family, and you see the look in their eyes. That's the trigger. Instantly, you feel that ball and twist in your gut as the automatic anxiety kicks in. The "monkey mind" takes over, a rambling storm of questions. Will they be okay? Will I be okay? What if I don't come back? What if I come back different? Fear, doubt, and confusion creep in, a suffocating fog.

I remember one departure. The final hugs were happening. I was supposed to be the strong one, the squared-away soldier. But inside, I was at war. My life with my family felt like it was over, and I was stepping into a future I couldn't predict. The noise of the hangar, the other families, it all started to fade.

All of a sudden, it hit me. A wave of panic. I felt light-headed, woozy, like I was going to pass out right there. I felt the jitters, and the hairs on my arms stood up. For a terrifying second, I felt like I was going to fall backwards, that the world was tilting off its axis. My mind was screaming, My life is over.

In that moment of freefall, a part of my training took over. I had to act. I quickly searched my mind, my surroundings, for something real. Anything. My hand was gripping the handle of my go-bag.

I focused on it. I squeezed it. I felt the cold, nylon texture of the handle. I felt its weight in my hand. I focused on it so intensely that for a single, intentional moment, it was the only thing in my universe.

And I felt the physical handle not just with my hands, but with my being.

That sensation provided the stability. The safety. The foundation that brought me back into focus. The storm in my head didn't vanish, but it subsided. The panic receded. I was back in my body, standing on solid ground, able to finish my goodbye with presence and strength, not just a brave face.

The Drill: The Lifeline Anchor

- **Mission Objective:** To interrupt a panic response during a peak moment of crisis.
- **Mission Time**: 10-15 Seconds
- **Recommended Frequency**: In any peak moment of crisis or overwhelming emotion, such as a difficult goodbye.

  - Find ONE physical sensation. It can be anything. The handle of your bag. The feeling of your boots pressed firmly on the pavement. The fabric of your child's coat as you hug them. The ring on your finger.
  - Bring one hundred percent of your attention to it.

Pour all of your focus into that single sensation for just three seconds. Feel its texture, its temperature, its weight.

- Breathe. Take one slow, deliberate breath, just like we practiced, while keeping your focus on that anchor.

That's it. This drill will not erase the sadness of leaving. It is not supposed to. Its mission is to interrupt the panic response. It pulls you out of the chaotic "what ifs" of the future and plants you firmly in the physical reality of the present moment. It gives you just enough solid ground to stand on, allowing you to act with courage and clarity, rather than being controlled by fear.

You can't control the future. You can't control the deployment. But in that moment, you can control your focus. And sometimes, that is everything.

Chapter 9: Staying Grounded in the Field - Practices for High-Stress Environments

The field is a different beast. Each place you go has its own personality, its own unique way of grinding you down. In Iraq, it was the heat and the sand. The heat was a physical presence, so oppressive it felt like you were taking a seat in hell. And the sand, a fine powder that got into everything—your gear, your food, your lungs. You'd have sandstorms that blotted out the sun, a kind of terror from above that left you disoriented and raw.

In environments like that, the biggest enemy isn't always outside the wire. It's the one inside your head.

During the long hours on watch, or the crushing boredom between missions, your mind can run adrift. You're exhausted, you're uncomfortable, and the questions start to creep in. Why did I choose this life? What am I even doing here? It's a dangerous spiral, a form of mission-dread that can corrode your focus, your morale, and your effectiveness.

I remember those moments vividly. I'd be standing post, the sun beating down, and my mind would just start to unravel. I'd question my whole life. But I learned that I could fight back, not by ignoring the misery, but by meeting it with a deliberate, two-part drill. It's a practice I came to rely on to find my ground when I felt like I was losing it.

The Drill: The Purpose Breath

- **Mission Objective**: To prepare your mind to be fully present for your team or family before a critical event
- **Mission Time**: 30-60 Seconds
- **Recommended Frequency**: As needed during long, difficult, or boring periods (e.g., on watch) to maintain focus and morale.

Step 1: Anchor with the Breath.

For thirty seconds, bring all your attention to the physical sensation of your breathing. Don't try to change it. Just notice it. Feel the air enter your nostrils, feel your chest expand, feel it leave your body. This is your anchor. It pulls your focus out of the chaotic "what-ifs" and firmly plants it in the physical reality of the present moment. You are here. You are breathing.

Step 2: Reorient with Your Purpose.

Once you have that moment of stillness, deliberately introduce a single thought—a piece of mental mission-briefing. The one I used was: "My action today will chart a better tomorrow. One day at a time."

Find the version that works for you. It could be: "I am here for the person standing next to me." Or "This moment will pass." Or simply, "Do your job."

This isn't about pretending you're not in a miserable situation. It's the opposite. It's about acknowledging the hardship and choosing to infuse it with purpose. It is a strategic reminder that your actions, right here, right now, have meaning. You are not just passively suffering; you are actively enduring. You are serving a mission.

Why It Works

This drill is effective because it tackles both the physiological and psychological aspects of stress. The breath interrupts the body's anxiety response. The mantra, or reframe, interrupts the mind's drift into hopelessness. It restores your sense of agency. You stop being a victim of your environment and reaffirm your role as a warrior within it.

Over a long deployment, it's this ability to manage the daily, grinding stress that separates the effective operator from the burnout case. Practicing the Purpose Breath won't make the heat go away or stop the sandstorms, but it will build your internal fortitude, allowing you to face the challenges with a clear mind and a steady hand. One day at a time.

Chapter 10: The Mindful Leader - Leading with Clarity and Composure

In the military, we're taught that leadership is about knowledge, tactics, and decisiveness. That's all true. But the most effective leaders I've ever known, the ones who could hold a team together in the worst of times, operated from a deeper principle: an inner human connection.

This connection is built on three pillars. Experience, which builds trust because your team knows you've walked the path. Courage, to face not only physical danger but the messy, human struggles that your people carry with them—because as the kids say, "life be lifing," even on deployment. And the most important pillar of all: Humility. The humility to see your team as human beings, to connect with them, and to show up for them in the way they need you to.

A leader's true test is how they behave when one of their own is broken. I saw this play out in stark reality during basic training.

We had a drill sergeant, DS Jones. He was a man who wanted to be feared—a true ass hole who seemed to enjoy being the meanest of them all. His leadership was built on intimidation, not inspiration. In our platoon was a trainee named Evans. One day, Evans received a letter from his wife telling him she was with someone else. He was heartbroken. In the pressure cooker of basic, it was too much. He wanted to quit, to go home, to do something. He was falling apart in front of us.

DS Jones saw his opening. With a sly smirk on his face, he leaned in and said, "Jodi's banging the hell out of her right now."

Evans broke. We all watched, a wave of disgust and anger washing over the platoon. In that single moment, DS Jones had shattered morale and lost any respect we might have had for him. He had used his power to inflict pain on the most vulnerable person in the room.

Just then, our Lieutenant, a tall, slender officer named Sanders, saw the commotion and walked over. He didn't yell. He didn't demand answers. He assessed the situation with his eyes. He took one look at Evans, who was completely undone, and called him over.

Gently, LT Sanders placed his left hand on Evans's shoulder. With his other hand, he put a finger under Evans's chin and raised his head, so they were looking eye-to-eye. He didn't say a word. But that one gesture—that simple, human act of connection and compassion—spoke volumes. It gave everyone who witnessed it a profound sense of humanity. It de-escalated the crisis. It showed respect to a man who had just been stripped of his dignity.

The story should have ended there, but it didn't. DS Jones, furious at the Lieutenant's intervention, took out his frustration on the rest of us. He barked at the team, and for the next hour, the PT was brutal as he punished us for his own lack of emotional control.

DS Jones was a reactive leader, run by his ego. LT Sanders was a mindful leader, guided by his humanity. A mindful leader understands that their internal state—their anger, their calm, their compassion—is not their own. It's a ripple that affects the entire team. They know that composure under pressure is a tactical asset.

The Drill: The Leader's Tactical Pause

- **Mission Objective**: To prepare your mind to be fully present for your team before a critical event
- **Mission Time**: 60 Seconds
- **Recommended Frequency**: Before any critical leadership event, such as giving a brief, starting a meeting, or having a difficult conversation.

  - Find Stillness. Stand or sit. Close your eyes or keep a soft gaze on the floor. Take three slow, deliberate breaths.
  - Check Your Internal Weather. Scan yourself. What are you feeling? Stressed? Tired? Annoyed? Impatient? Acknowledge it without judgment. Naming it prevents it from unconsciously leaking out and contaminating your team's climate.
  - Consider Your People. Bring your team to mind. Who is struggling? Who is excelling? What challenges are they facing outside of the mission? This is the humility piece—seeing them as whole people.
  - Set Your Intention. Silently state your intention. "My mission is to lead with clarity and composure." "I will

be present for my team." "I will listen."

This practice isn't about being soft. It is the ultimate act of operational control, starting with the most important asset you have: your own mind. It's how you become the leader who sees the human being inside the uniform and knows, like LT Sanders, that sometimes the most powerful action is a quiet gesture of support.

Chapter 11: Maintaining Connection - Meditations for While You're Away

A long deployment creates a mental drain like no other. You are living in what feels like a different dimension, a different reality from the people you love. The longer you're gone, the wider that dimensional gap becomes. And the powerful, overwhelming emotions of love and connection that you started with can, despite your best efforts, begin to decline.
It's not because you love them any less. It's because the shared world you inhabited with them is gone. In a way, it feels like losing a battle buddy.

You share so many moments, so many routines, so much of your life with someone, and then one day, they are simply not there. You're left with the ghost of that connection. Every day is difficult. You see something that reminds you of them—a song, a photo, a memory that pops into your head for no reason—and you feel that sharp pang of loss. It's the pain of a connection that feels like it's in the past tense.

If you just let this happen, the connection can fade. The difficult moments can curdle into resentment or apathy. But you can choose to engage. You can choose to turn those painful moments into a practice of active connection. It's a drill built on two commands: Honor, and Reframe.

The Drill: The Connection Drill

- **Mission Objective**: To transform moments of loneliness

into a active practice of connection.

- **Mission Time**: 1-2 Minutes
- **Recommended Frequency**: As needed when memories or feelings of loneliness arise during a long separation.

Step 1: Honor the Moment.

When a memory of a loved one arises, don't shove it down. Stop what you're doing, even if just for five seconds. Close your eyes if you can. Bring the memory fully to your mind—their face, their laugh, the feeling of holding their hand. Acknowledge the feeling that comes with it, whether it's sadness, love, or longing. Just let it be there. You are honoring the reality and power of that connection. You are saying, "This matters. You matter."

Step 2: Reframe with Purpose

After holding that memory and feeling for a moment, introduce a deliberate reframe. You are giving the pain of the present a purpose for the future. Silently say to yourself, or to the person in your memory:

"I get to be with you again. The work I am doing now is shaping a life where I never have to leave your side again."

Find your own words, but make them about the future. You are transforming the pain of absence into the fuel for reunion. You are not just a passive victim of the distance; you are an active architect of your future life together.

Why It Works

This practice won't eliminate the difficulty of separation. But over time, the difficult moments will slowly fade. They will become less hurtful because you have consistently met them with love and purpose. You are not just waiting for the deployment to end; you are actively carrying your connection through the fire, ready to be reunited, stronger and more committed than before.

Chapter 12: The Post-Deployment Debrief - Processing a Return

Coming home is not the end of the mission. In many ways, it's the beginning of a new, more complex one. You can't just take off the uniform and expect the warrior inside you to disappear. He came home with you. The final, and perhaps most crucial, part of any deployment is conducting a thorough after-action debrief on yourself to understand what you brought back.

Let me be straight with you. Even today, thirty years after I left the military, even after becoming a certified mindfulness and meditation teacher, there is one thing I still can't do.

I can't sit with my back to a door.

If I walk into a restaurant or a meeting room and the only available seat faces the wall, something in me activates. It's a creature. The anxiety kicks in, and the Incredible Hulk shows up, hijacking my entire experience. All my focus, all my energy, gets sucked into that feeling of being exposed, of not having eyes on the exits. My "Commander in the HQ" goes offline, and the big green guy is in charge.

Now, with my training, I can use mindfulness in that moment. I can acknowledge the feeling. I can observe it. But here's the truth: The acknowledgment doesn't make it leave. The Hulk is still there, wanting to smash.

The anxiety, the "Hulk," only recedes and returns to being

David Banner when I make a tactical adjustment—when I move to a place where I can see the layout of the room.

This is the reality of the post-deployment debrief. It's not about "fixing" yourself or erasing these responses. It's about first identifying what your triggers are—what brings your "Hulk" out. And second, it's about developing a clear plan to manage that reality with calm, strategic action instead of panicked reaction. The goal isn't to pretend you don't have a Hulk. The goal is to become a very self-aware David Banner.

The Drill: The "Acknowledge and Adapt" Debrief

- **Mission Objective**: To manage hyper-vigilant responses with strategic action instead of panicked reaction.
- **Mission Time**: Under 1 Minute
- **Recommended Frequency**: Every time you notice a known trigger (like your back to a door) causing a hyper-vigilant response.

  - *Identify the Trigger.* The first step is simple observation. What just happened? I sat with my back to the door. I heard a loud bang. Someone came up behind me too quickly. Just notice the event without judgment. This is your intel report.
  - *Acknowledge the "Hulk".* As the feeling rises, name it internally. "Okay, the Hulk is here. I feel that anxiety in my gut. I feel my heart rate kicking up." Don't fight it. Don't get angry at yourself. You are simply acknowledging the presence of a powerful force. This is the moment of mindfulness.

- ***Take a Tactical Pause.*** Before you do anything, take one, slow, deliberate breath. Use the Box Breathing we practiced. This one breath is you, as David Banner, putting a hand on the Hulk's shoulder and saying, "I got this." It gives your "Commander in HQ" a split second to come back online.
- ***Adapt Your Environment.*** This is not an act of weakness; it is an act of superior strategy. Based on the intel you've gathered, make a calm adjustment. Move your seat. Step outside for a minute. Put on your headphones. You are not running from a threat. You are tactically repositioning to create the conditions for your own peace of mind.

Coming home is a process of learning the new landscape of yourself. There will be parts of you that are forever changed by your service. The debrief is about honoring that reality. You learn your triggers, you acknowledge the power of the responses they create, and you develop calm, effective strategies to navigate the world as the person you are now.

PART IV: FOR THE VETERAN - ON THE HOME FRONT

Chapter 13: The Transition - Navigating a World That Doesn't Speak Your Language

No one tells you that one of your hardest assignments will come after you take off the uniform for the last time. The transition back to civilian life is a mission with no brief, no map, and no clear objective. You step out of the military—a true container where you understood the rules and your place in the world—and you find yourself a stranger in your own home.

I remember that feeling like it was yesterday. It was like being a fish out of water. The people, the pace, the priorities—everything felt foreign. Even my own family, the people I loved most, didn't fully get the ways I had changed. They couldn't understand the conditioning. To this day, my body still wakes up at 5:30 AM, no alarm needed. The system established in me is permanent.

But nowhere was the culture shock more jarring than in the civilian workplace.

I was frustrated beyond belief. My peers' work habits felt grotesque, appallingly lazy. The lack of urgency, the sloppy standards, the different definition of a "full day's work"—it drove me crazy. I found myself becoming aggressive in my stance, constantly complaining, my body tight with aggravation. I was judging them against the standards of a world they'd never known, and the frustration was eating me alive.

Think back to a soldier like Trainee Evans from Basic—the one who got the Dear John letter. We all knew guys like him. What happens to a soldier like that when they get out? The world hits them hard. Without the structure of the military, that heartbreak and anger can become a defining part of their transition. They might struggle to trust new people, carry a chip on their shoulder, or look for that feeling of betrayal around every corner. Their 'war within' didn't start downrange; it started with a letter in a barracks. Helping guys like him starts with understanding that.

In those moments of anger, I had to learn a new kind of discipline. I had to create a new drill, not for the battlefield, but for the breakroom. It was a practice of breathing through the aggravation and deliberately reframing the situation.

The Drill: The Transition Reframe

- **Mission Objective**: To transform feeling of frustration with the civilian world into gratitude and acceptance.
- **Mission Time**: 30 Seconds
- **Recommended Frequency**: As needed in moments of frustration or "culture shock" when interacting with the civilian world.

  - **Breathe Through It**. The moment you feel that heat rising in your chest, that frustration tightening your gut, that is your signal. Before you speak, before you react, take one conscious, tactical breath. Just one. This isn't to make the feeling go away; it's to create enough space so you are in command, not your anger.

- **State the Reality**. In your mind, state the simple truth: "I am not in the military anymore." This isn't a statement of loss. It is a reorientation to your new environment, like checking your compass. You are acknowledging the new rules of engagement.

- **Execute the Reframe**. This is the key maneuver. Instead of judging them by your standards, you reframe the situation with understanding and gratitude. Tell yourself: "They have not been trained and improved in the way that I have. I was blessed to have received that training."

This simple shift in perspective is monumental. It moves you from a place of resentful judgment to a place of quiet pride and compassion. You stop seeing them as lazy and start seeing yourself as fortunate. You transform a source of endless frustration into a moment of gratitude for the discipline and strength that was forged in you.

Why It Works

This practice isn't about lowering your standards. It's about preserving your own peace of mind. You cannot change the civilian world to meet military standards, and trying to will only exhaust and embitter you.

The Transition Reframe allows you to hold onto the best parts of your conditioning—your discipline, your drive, your high standards—without letting them become a weapon you use against yourself and others. It's how you navigate this new world, not as an angry and alienated outsider, but as a seasoned veteran who has the wisdom to adapt and overcome any challenge, including the challenge of coming home.

Chapter 14: Scanning Your Inner Sector - A Body Scan for Hypervigilance

In the service, you became an expert at scanning your sector. Your life, and the lives of your team, depended on your ability to be constantly aware of your surroundings. You could visually account for every inch within your purview, mentally calculating and determining risk levels in a split second. It's a skill forged in high-stakes environments.

The problem is that for many of us, the scanner stays on. Years after leaving the service, we still find ourselves scanning every room we enter. Our bodies stay clenched, ready for a threat that is no longer there. This state of constant, low-level readiness is called hypervigilance. It's the clenched jaw, the shoulders that live up by your ears, the inability to ever truly feel at ease. It is exhausting.

This chapter is about taking your elite skill of threat assessment and turning it inward. I want you to take that same focus, that same tenacity you used to scan a perimeter, and use it to scan your own body. We are going on an internal scouting mission.

The Drill: The Inner Sector Scan

- **Mission Objective**: To gather intelligence on your physical state and give your body the "all clear" signal to release tension.
- **Mission Time**: 5-10 Minutes
- **Recommended Frequency**: A few times a week, or

nightly before sleep, to release accumulated physical tension.

Find a comfortable place to sit where you won't be disturbed for a few minutes. Close your eyes if you are comfortable doing so.

- **Begin the Scan**. Bring your awareness to the very top of your head. Just like starting a patrol from a designated point, this is your rally point.
- **Move Inward.** Slowly begin your scan downward, moving with the pace of your breath. Scan your forehead and your eyes. Are they tight? Furrowed? Just notice. This is your intel.
- **Scan Your Jaw and Neck**. This is an area where stress loves to hide. Is your jaw clenched? Are your teeth grinding? Just observe. Breathe into that sector.
- **Proceed to the Shoulders and Arms**. Scan down your shoulders. Are they tense and raised, ready for a fight? Let your scan move down your arms to your hands. Are your fists clenched? Just take note.
- **Sweep the Torso**. Scan your chest and your gut. Is there a tightness there? A knot of anxiety? Remember, you are just scouting. You are not engaging, just observing. Breathe.
- **Scan the Legs and Feet**. Continue the patrol down through your legs, your calves, all the way to the soles of your feet. Feel them connected to the ground. This is your entire area of operations.

You have now completed a full scan of your inner sector. You have a complete intelligence picture of where your body is holding tension.

The "All Clear" Signal

Think about being on a tense patrol. You are on high alert, scanning everything, muscles tight. Then, the assessment is over. You realize there is no enemy, there is no immediate risk. What does your body do? It relaxes. It lets go of that tension. It gives that deep sigh of relief—that "woosaaa."

The same thing happens when you do this inner scan. By methodically assessing every part of your body for the "enemy" of tension, you are showing your nervous system that there is no true, physical threat right now. The tightness you feel is just a leftover echo from past battles. As you notice this, as you breathe into it, you give your body permission to stand down. You give it the "all clear."

Pay attention to your body. It is always giving you signals. It's telling you when there is an inner risk, a foreign invader like chronic dis-ease. Learning to read those signals is the first step to taking command of your own well-being.

Chapter 15: Setting Down the Rucksack - Working with Memories and Moral Injury

Of all the weight we carry in our rucksacks after service, the heaviest components are the memories. For a long time after I came home, these memories were the predator, and I was their hostage.

They would come from nowhere, sneaking up on me when I was least prepared. A specific scent or a loud noise would open the floodgates, and I would be right back there. With the memories came the guilt—the crushing, suffocating guilt of being alive when so many of my friends didn't make it. The feeling of not being worthy to be alive, that it should have been me instead.

With the guilt came the pain of the loss itself. Not just the loss of a person, but the loss of the conversations we shared, the connection, the future that was stolen from them.

I didn't know how to carry it. So, I tried to numb it. I drank a lot to drown the pain of all the unhealed trauma I experienced in my life. I engaged in risky behaviors, things that degraded the man I had fought to become. I was a ticking time bomb of unresolved grief and guilt, and the fuse was getting shorter.

The rucksack we carry is filled with our own experiences, but it's also filled with the ghosts of others. It holds the memory of DS Jones's cruelty and the quiet dignity of LT Sanders. It holds the face of Trainee Evans, a reminder that some of the deepest wounds we see are inflicted not by the enemy, but by life itself. Honoring our own journey requires us to acknowledge the impact of theirs on our own path.

After many arguments with my wife, it finally happened. I fell asleep at the wheel and got a DUI.

That was my rock bottom. That was the moment I knew. I had to stop running. I had to turn and face what was chasing me. I made a decision: I have to conquer this demon and begin the inner healing. For me, that path forward was a combination of therapy and the daily practice of meditation.

The work isn't about forgetting. You cannot and should not forget those you lost. The work is about changing your relationship with the memories. It's about learning to set the rucksack down, look at what's inside with courage, and choose to carry it with honor, not with shame. The practice below is a formal way to do that. It is a way to honor the fallen and, in doing so, reclaim your own life.

The Drill: The Honoring Practice

- **Mission Objective**: To safely process grief and transform a painful memory into a sacred duty.
- **Mission Time**: 5-10 Minutes
- **Recommended Frequency**: This is a formal practice, not a daily drill. Use it intentionally when you feel ready to process grief in a safe space.

- **Find Your Anchor**. Before you begin, ground yourself firmly in the present moment. Feel your feet flat on the floor. Take several slow, deliberate breaths. Remind yourself: "I am safe. I am here, now." You are creating a safe container from which to view the memory, so you are the observer, not the hostage.

- **Gently Call a Memory to Mind.** This is not about reliving trauma. It is about connection. Gently bring to mind the face of a person you lost. See their smile. Remember a good moment, a shared laugh, the feeling of brotherhood.

- **Acknowledge the Feelings**. As you hold this memory, feelings will arise—grief, love, sadness, maybe even anger. Your job is not to fight them. Just acknowledge them. Silently say to yourself, "This is grief. This is love." Let the feelings be there, like weather passing through.

- **Make the Honorable Vow.** With the memory of your friend in your mind and the feelings in your body, silently make this vow to them. Use these words, or find your own that carry the same weight: "Even though you are not here, I will never forget you. I will always honor your memory as long as I'm alive."

- **Connect Your Life to Their Memory**. Now, add the final, crucial step. You give their memory a new purpose, and you give your life a renewed mission. Silently add: "I will live my life in a way that is worthy of the gift of life I still have. I will carry your memory with honor."

- **Return to Your Anchor.** To close the practice, bring your full attention back to your breath. Back to your feet on the floor. Take a few more deep breaths. You have successfully set the rucksack down, honored its contents, and chosen to pick it back up with strength and purpose.

This practice transforms a memory from a predator that attacks you into a sacred duty you choose to uphold. The pain of the loss doesn't vanish, but its nature changes. It becomes a source of strength, a reminder of your most solemn mission: to live a life of honor for those who cannot.

Chapter 16: Finding Your New Mission - Re-establishing Purpose and Identity

If you're reading this chapter hoping for a secret map that leads to your one true purpose in life, I need to start with the honest truth. It's good to hear you think I've made it. But truth is, there are days that I still feel off kilter. My process of finding myself was, and still is, a journey.

There is no final destination where you arrive and say, "I've found it, I am now complete." There is only the path, and learning to walk it with intention.

In the service, you always know the mission. You may not know every single detail of what's coming, but you know your part. You know your objective, and you have trained relentlessly on how to execute your role. There is a profound clarity and sense of identity in that. You are a soldier, a warrior, a member of a team, and this is your mission.

Returning to society is a shock to the system because that clarity vanishes overnight. Suddenly, there is no mission brief. There is no defined objective. There is no clear identity. You feel adrift, and that feeling is dangerous. It can lead to the darkness we talked about in the last chapter.

When I first faced this void, my first mission wasn't grand or glorious. It wasn't about changing the world. It had to be simpler than that. I realized my first mission was just to build a life. I wanted to get a job. I wanted to be married, have children, a house, and a dog.

I found my new purpose by doing something incredibly simple. I started to just write down what I wanted to accomplish in my life. I gave myself a new mission to live for, written by my own hand. This is your first drill in finding your new way forward.

The Drill: Your Written Mission Brief

- **Mission Objective**: To create clarity and direction for your new civilian life.
- **Mission Time**: 10-15 Minutes to create; 1 minute to review.
- **Recommended Frequency**: Create the brief once. Review it daily or weekly to maintain focus. Update it quarterly or as your missions change.

  - **Get Your Gear**. Find a quiet moment. Take out a blank piece of paper and a pen.
  - **Write Your Objectives**. At the top of the page, write "Mission Objectives." Now, just start writing your answers to these simple questions. Don't judge them. Don't worry if they seem too small or too big. Just write.
    - ✓ What does a stable life look like for me right now?
    - ✓ What is one thing I want to accomplish in the next month?
    - ✓ What is one thing I want to accomplish in the next year?
    - ✓ What kind of person do I want to be for my

family and friends?

✓ What is one thing, just for me, that would bring me a sense of peace or satisfaction?

▪ **Post Your Orders.** Take this piece of paper and put it somewhere you will see it every day. On your bathroom mirror. On the dashboard of your truck. On your refrigerator. This is not a list of dreams; this is your new set of orders.

Why It Works

In the service, your mission gives you direction. It tells you where to put your energy. This written mission brief does the same thing for your civilian life. It cuts through the confusion and gives you a clear target to aim for.

Your mission will change as you change. You will accomplish things on your list, and new objectives will arise. Maybe your first mission is just "Get a job that pays the bills." Once that's accomplished, your next mission might be "Find a career that I don't hate." And later, it might become "Find work that helps others."

This is the journey. You don't find your purpose once. You build it, mission by mission, one objective at a time. The first step is simply to decide what today's mission is, and write it down.

Chapter 17: Dealing with the Darkness - Mindfulness for Anxiety and Depression

Before we begin this chapter, a critical mission brief: Depression and anxiety are real, clinical conditions. The mindfulness practices in this book are powerful tools in your kit, but they are meant to be used alongside, not as a replacement for, professional help. Seeking therapy or medicine is not a sign of weakness; it is a sign of immense strength and a strategic move to get the support you have earned. My own healing journey included both therapy and meditation.

Now, let's talk about the fight. There's a difference between a bad day and the "Darkness." The Darkness of depression is a weight. It's a thick, heavy fog that smothers motivation, drains your energy, and tells you that you are worthless. The Darkness of anxiety is a frantic, chaotic storm of "what-ifs" that hijacks your mind and puts your body in a constant state of high alert. These are two different enemies, and they require different tactics.

Fighting the Fog of Depression: The Power of the Next Right Action

I remember a deep depression I went through after my service. I couldn't find a job. For two years, I sent out countless resumes and went on interviews, but nothing. The weight of it was crushing. I didn't feel like a man. I had a child to support, a wife who was losing faith in me, and I felt like I could not catch a break. The fog was so thick I didn't know what to do with myself. I felt like my life was over. I didn't just want to be out of my situation; I didn't want to be here on this earth at all.

One of the most dangerous things about depression is that it paralyzes you. The weight feels so immense that doing anything at all seems impossible. The key is to find the smallest possible action and execute it.

For me, that action was taking a job at McDonald's. To some, that might have looked like a step down, a failure. But for me, it was a declaration of war against the fog. It was an action. It was forward movement.

And I made a choice. While I was there, I would be present. I was "happy smiling" as I served customers. People didn't know my story; they just saw a man choosing his attitude. That single, humble action created momentum. I got promoted to manager, then worked my way up to a district manager role. I continued to push forward because deep down, I held on to a single belief: I knew I was called to a higher place.

The Drill: The Next Right Action

- **Mission Objective**: To fight the paralysis of depression by building momentum through small, mindful actions.
- **Mission Time:** Varies (from 30 seconds to 5 minutes per action).
- **Recommended Frequency**: As needed in moments of depressive paralysis to build momentum.

- **Acknowledge the Weight**. First, acknowledge the reality without judgment. "Okay. The depression is heavy today. It feels like I'm moving through mud."
- **Identify ONE Action**. Your mission is to identify the absolute smallest, most manageable next right action. Not "solve my problems," but "get out of bed." Not "clean the whole house," but "put one dish in the sink." Not "find my dream career," but "take a shower."
- **Execute with Full Attention.** Pour all of your focus into that one action. If you're taking a shower, feel the water on your skin. If you're making coffee, smell the grounds. If you're tying your boots, feel the laces in your hands. For those few moments, your entire world is that one simple task. You are not thinking about the past or worrying about the future. You are just here, now, taking action.

One small action builds momentum for the next one. This is how you fight the paralysis of depression. You prove to yourself, one step at a time, that you can still move forward.

Breaking the Spiral of Anxiety

Anxiety is a different enemy. It's not a lack of energy, but a frantic excess of it, a "what-if" spiral that takes over your mind. When you feel that storm starting, your go-to drill should be the 5-4-3-2-1 Anchoring Technique we learned in Chapter 6.

Anxiety lives in the future, in the catastrophic "what-ifs." The

5-4-3-2-1 drill forces your mind out of that imaginary future and plants it firmly in the physical reality of the present moment. It is the fastest way to break the spiral and get your Commander back in the HQ.

The Darkness is a formidable opponent, but it is not invincible. By meeting it with the right tools—the mindful action for depression, the aggressive grounding for anxiety—you can learn to navigate the storm, one moment at a time.

Winning this war within isn't a mission you have to complete alone. The next section is for the most important member of your fire team: your family. I encourage you to share it with them, as their understanding and support are critical to your success.

PART V: FOR THE HOME TEAM - SUPPORTING THE MISSION

Chapter 18: For Spouses & Partners - Finding Your Own Standstill in the Chaos

This chapter is for the silent ranks of the military community, the husbands, wives, and partners who serve in a unique and demanding role. You are the anchor, the constant in a world of chaos, the person who holds everything together back home. But who holds you?

The life of a military partner is a masterclass in managing the unknown. You wrestle with a constant, low-level fear for your partner's safety—their physical and mental well-being. You deal with the profound loneliness of deployment, the stress of frequent moves, and the challenge of putting your own career and dreams on hold. You live with an uncertainty that is not your own, yet it dictates your life.

Amidst all this, one of the biggest struggles is the loss of your own identity. It's easy to feel like your entire life is defined by your supporting role. Like the veteran returning to civilian life, you can begin to ask, "Who am I? What is my mission? Where do I fit into this picture?"

In my work with military families, the first and most important conversation I have with a spouse or partner is about them as an individual. Before you can be the rock for your family, you must find your own solid ground. You cannot pour from an empty cup. This chapter is about how to start filling your own tank, so you have the strength and water in the well to draw from when your family needs you most.

I once worked with a spouse who felt she had completely lost herself. The constant stress and uncertainty of her husband's deployments had brought her to what she described as the "break of insanity." She had no control over anything in her life, and she was drowning. Her journey back to herself didn't start with a grand gesture. It started with one, small, controllable action. She began volunteering at a local food bank for a few hours a week.

Why did this work? Because it gave her something the military life had taken away: a sense of consistency, a tangible value for her time, and the immediate result of seeing her actions make a difference. In a world of chaos, this simple act provided the physical and mental safety her mind desperately needed. It was her own mission. Combined with a simple yoga practice, she found she could show up better at home because she was finally showing up for herself.

Finding your own "food bank"—that small, controllable thing that gives you purpose—is the key.

The Drill: The Compass Drill - Finding Your True North

- **Mission Objective**: To reconnect with your own needs and desires, separate from your supporting role.
- **Mission Time**: 10 Minutes
- **Recommended Frequency**: Weekly or monthly as an act of self-care and to check in with yourself.

  - **Breathe.** Take three slow, deep breaths. With each exhale, imagine letting go of one responsibility, one worry, one role. Let yourself just be a person, not a spouse, not a parent, just you.

- **Answer the Prompts.** Write down your honest answers to these questions. Don't judge them. Just listen to what comes up.
  - ✓ What is one thing I used to love doing before this life took over?
  - ✓ If I had one hour this week that was one hundred percent mine, what would I do with it?
  - ✓ What is one small thing I can do today that would make me feel strong or capable?
  - ✓ What is a subject or skill I've always been curious about?
  - ✓ What does my body need right now? (e.g., rest, a walk, stretching, quiet).
- **Choose One Action**. Look at your list. Choose one small, achievable action you can take this week. Just one. That is your new personal mission objective.

Why It Works

This practice is an act of self-love and ownership over your own happiness. By mindfully identifying your own burning desires and taking small actions to honor them, you begin to fill your own cup.

When your cup is full, you are not just surviving; you are thriving. You can give to your family from a place of abundance, not depletion. You show up with more patience, more resilience, and more strength. You are not just the support for the mission; you are a vital, whole, and powerful part of the team, with a clear direction for your own compass.

Chapter 19: Meditations for Military Families - Staying Connected Through Moves and Deployments

The military doesn't just recruit a service member; it recruits an entire family. You are all part of the mission, and you all face the consequences of a life defined by upheaval. The two greatest challenges to a family unit are the chaos of a Permanent Change of Station (PCS) and the long, lonely separation of a deployment.

During these times, it is easy for a family to fracture under the stress. You become a collection of individuals trying to survive your own private turmoil, living like roommates in the same house. Communication breaks down. Tempers get short. The connection that makes a family strong begins to fray.

The most powerful way to protect your family's connection is to build shared rituals of mindfulness. Now, this does not mean you need to get your children to sit on a cushion for twenty minutes. A family's mindfulness practice is about one thing: intentionally carving out time to build intimacy and create a safe space for communication.

It's about creating a predictable, safe harbor where every member of the family feels seen, heard, and valued. It's a way to build intimacy and keep the lines of communication open, especially when life feels chaotic and uncertain.

The Drill: The Family Connection Rituals

- **Mission Objective**: To build family intimacy and create a safe space for communication.
- **Mission Time**: 15-20 Minutes
- **Recommended Frequency**: Once a week, consistently, to build a strong family habit.

1. The Weekly "What's On Your Mind?" Meeting.

This is a simple, powerful tool. Once a week—maybe Sunday evening after dinner—the family gathers for a fifteen-minute check-in. The rules are simple and must be respected to create a safe space:

> *One person shares at a time*. The job of everyone else is to listen with their full attention—no phones, no interruptions.
>
> *Confirm Completion*. To ensure the person has said everything they need to, the speaker can say, "I'm complete," when they are finished. Alternatively, the parent or facilitator can gently ask, "Are you complete?" This respectfully signals that it is the next person's turn.
>
> *Listen to understand, don't listen to "fix."* For parents especially, the instinct is to jump in and solve a child's problem. Resist this. After someone has shared something difficult, a much more powerful question is: "Thank you for sharing that. Is there anything here you desire me to act on?" This gives them agency. Often, people don't need a solution; they just need to be

heard.

2. The Mindful Walk.

Once a week, go for a twenty-minute family walk. The only rule: for the first ten minutes, everyone leaves their phone behind and focuses on the walk itself. Pay attention to the sights and sounds around you. Talk about what you see. The second ten minutes can be for open conversation. This simple act of sharing a distraction-free experience together rebuilds connection in a quiet, natural way.

3. The Mindful Movie Night.
Choose one night a week for a family movie. But do it with intention. Make popcorn. Turn off all the phones and put them in a different room. The mindfulness is in the shared focus, in laughing together, in experiencing the same story as a team. It's a simple way to create a positive, shared memory during a stressful time.

Why It Works

These simple, consistent rituals are anchors in the storm of military life. For a child dealing with a new school or a deployed parent, knowing that every Sunday night they will have a chance to be heard—truly and completely heard—can be a lifeline. For a couple strained by the stress of a move, a quiet walk can be the only time they truly connect all week.

You are building a resilient family culture. You are teaching your children, by example, how to communicate with respect and intention. And most importantly, you are carving out sacred time to remind yourselves that you are not just a collection of individuals under one roof—you are a family, a team, connected and strong, ready to face any mission together.

Chapter 20: The Bridge Home - A Guide for Supporting Your Veteran's Transition

Your partner is home. The deployment is over, the transition is official, and the person you love is back in your life. This is the moment you've been waiting for. But it can also be one of the most confusing and difficult times for a relationship.

There is a blind spot that many partners have, and it is the source of immense, unintentional pain. It is the expectation that the person who returned is the exact same person who left.

They may look the same. They may sound the same. But the person who served, especially in a combat zone, has had experiences that are now engrained in their being. For decades, the military didn't encourage or foster the tools for service members to process these experiences. So your partner may have come home with a rucksack full of memories, grief, and hyper-vigilance, and no idea how to unpack it.

Your role in this is not to be their therapist or to "fix" them. That is not your job. Your mission, should you choose to accept it, is to be the Bridge Home. A bridge doesn't force someone across; it simply provides a safe, stable path. Your role is to be the loving, patient architect of the safe space your veteran needs to begin their own journey of healing. So, how do you build that bridge?

A Note from the Home Front

By Karen Irick

To the partner reading this, who stands on the other side of that bridge waiting for your veteran to cross back home—I see you. And I understand. When Demetrius was transitioning, I learned that my most difficult and important mission was to constantly show the man I loved that he was worthy. It was to be a mirror that reflected his value back to him when the memories and the guilt were telling him he didn't deserve happiness or love.

If I could give you one piece of advice, it would be to wrap yourself in patience. This road is not an easy one, but I can tell you with certainty that if your partner is willing to do the work alongside you, it will get better. You cannot do the work for them, but you can create the safe space for them to do it in. Learn to appreciate the small wins—a moment of shared laughter, a quiet conversation that feels like old times, a single good day. These are not small things. They are monumental victories on the path home.

As for your own strength, you must find what fills your cup. For me, it was my faith and spirituality. It was also the practical understanding that a strong marriage is work. It isn't a fairy tale; it is a partnership built on good days and bad days. Releasing the pressure of "perfection" allows you to build something real and resilient.

Your love is a powerful, healing force. Your patience is a gift.

And your own well-being is the foundation of the home your veteran is fighting to return to.

The Bridge Builder's Toolkit

These are not rules, but tools. They are actions you can take to create an environment of patience, understanding, and healing.

1. Create Space with Your Words.

Your veteran may feel disoriented, out of place, and pressured to be "back to normal." You can relieve that pressure with simple, powerful words. Try saying something like: "I am so glad you are home. I know this is a big shift, and I want you to know it's okay to take the space and time you need to process everything. We'll figure out this new normal together." This single statement can feel like a lifeline, giving them permission to be where they are, not where they think they should be.

2. Gently Re-establish Routines

The military runs on routine. The civilian world can feel chaotic in comparison. You can help ground your veteran by gently and collaboratively incorporating small, stable routines into your daily life. This isn't about creating a rigid schedule, but about providing anchors of normalcy. It could be as simple as making coffee together every morning, taking a short walk after dinner, or committing to a family meal with no phones. These small rituals create a sense of predictability and safety.

3. Encourage, Don't Push

Invite your veteran back into the fold of family life without making it a demand. The key is gentle encouragement. "I'm heading to our son's school event, I'd love for you to come if you're up for it." "I'm working on that project you were interested in, want to take a look?" This encourages their participation in household activities, school events, and their own burning desires, signaling that they are a wanted and needed part of the team.

4. Rebuild Intimacy in Layers.

As we've discussed, intimacy is more than just physical. It's about shared experiences. Use the Family Connection Rituals from the last chapter to rebuild your bond as a team. A movie night, a shared walk, a "What's On Your Mind?" meeting— these are the building blocks of a deep, resilient connection that can withstand the aftershocks of deployment.

The Most Important Rule: Protect Your Own Well-being

We will end this section where we started it: you cannot pour from an empty cup. To be a strong and stable bridge for your partner, you must continue to practice your own self-love and mindfulness. Your well-being is not selfish; it is a critical component of your family's overall readiness and health. You are not just supporting the mission; you are the mission.

PART VI: THE DEBRIEF - MAINTAINING YOUR PRACTICE

Chapter 21: Field-Stripping Your Habits - Making Mindfulness a Lifelong Skill

You have now worked your way through this entire guide. You have learned the science, practiced the core skills, and explored how these tools can be applied to every phase of your life—from active duty, to the veteran's journey, to your role within your family.

But the greatest challenge is not learning these skills. The greatest challenge is maintaining them for a lifetime. After the initial motivation fades, it is easy to get caught up again in the endless civilian mission of "the doing." The job, the bills, the family obligations, the stresses of daily life—they all demand your attention. In that storm of activity, many of us lose focus on the one thing that allows us to handle it all: ourselves. We stop making ourselves the mission.

After all the missions you have been assigned, there is one final mission that lasts a lifetime: YOU.

You are the single most important asset you have. Your well-being, your clarity, and your inner peace are the foundation upon which everything else is built. To be the best husband, father, wife, mother, employee, or leader you can be, you must first operate at your optimal self. You must show up for yourself before you can effectively show up for anyone else.

Our society often gets this backwards. It teaches us that focusing on ourselves is selfish. I am telling you today that we must re-evaluate that word. It is not selfish to ensure your own internal readiness. It is a fundamental responsibility. As the old saying goes, you must sweep your own front porch before you can worry about your neighbor's. Taking ownership of your healing, your thoughts, and your life is the ultimate act of personal responsibility. You can't help anyone until you first help yourself. You can't pour from an empty cup.

So, how do we maintain this practice for life? We field-strip it down to its most essential component.

When you strip away all the different drills and techniques in this book, you are left with one non-negotiable component: The daily habit of checking in with yourself.

The Drill: The Daily Self-Debrief

- **Mission Objective**: To make your own well-being a non-negotiable, daily mission.
- **Mission Time**: 5 Minutes
- **Recommended Frequency**: Daily. Non-negotiable.

  - **Establish Your Time.** First thing in the morning is best, before the day's chaos begins. But any time you can consistently commit to is the right time.
  - **Find Stillness**. Sit in a quiet place. You don't need a special cushion. A chair, the edge of your bed, even your truck before you walk into work. Just be still.
  - **Ask the Question**. Close your eyes, take three slow breaths, and ask yourself one simple, honest question: ***"What do I need today?"***

- **Listen for the Answer**. Just listen. Don't judge the answer. The answer might be "quiet." It might be "a phone call with a friend." It might be "a healthy meal," "a walk outside," or "ten minutes to just be left alone." The answer might be "help." Whatever it is, it is your truth for that day.
- **Commit to One Action.** Based on the answer, make a silent commitment to take one small action today to honor that need. If you need quiet, commit to taking a ten-minute walk by yourself. If you need connection, commit to sending that text message.

This simple, five-minute practice is the field-stripped version of it all. It ensures that no matter how busy or stressful life gets, you start every single day by reporting for duty to your most important mission: your own well-being. This is the foundation for a healthy society, and it is the key to a life of purpose and peace.

Chapter 22: Continuing the Mission - Resources and Next Steps

We have come to the end of this field guide, but not to the end of your journey. The final page of a book is often seen as an ending, but I want you to see this as the beginning of your next mission. You have been given a set of tools, a new perspective, and a framework for your Mental

PT. Now, the real work begins.

I want to leave you, and your family, with one final message.

Welcome home, soldier.

Thank you, family, friends, and loved ones, for your service. The new mission is building a life of practices, tiny habits built on the need, desire, and respect for the life you have now. Make the best of each day. You know what a process it has been to be here today... You have the proof... you are encoded with greatness. You have all you need to be successful.

The mission of living well is not one you have to undertake alone. A core principle of military life is knowing when to call for support. Below is a list of logistical and professional resources available to you. Using them is a sign of strength. It is you, the Commander of your own life, calling in the right assets for the mission.

Essential Resources for the Continuing Mission

Disclaimer: This is not an exhaustive list, but a starting point for exploring the support available to you.

For Immediate Support
- **Veterans Crisis Line**: If you are in crisis or having thoughts of suicide, do not wait. Confidential help is available twenty-four hours a day, seven days a week.
  - *Dial 988 and then Press 1*
  - *Text 838255*
  - *Chat online at VeteransCrisisLine.net*

U.S. Department of Veterans Affairs (VA) Resources
- **Main Information Hub (VA.gov):** This is the primary source for all information on VA benefits, including healthcare, education, and disability claims.
  - Website: https://www.VA.gov
- **VA Mental Health Services:** The VA provides a wide range of mental health services specifically tailored for veterans. You can learn about treatment options for PTSD, depression, anxiety, and more.
  - Website: https://www.mentalhealth.va.gov
- **Vet Centers**: These are community-based counseling centers that provide free and confidential social and psychological services to veterans and their families. They are less formal than a large VA hospital and are staffed by many veterans. They are an excellent resource for readjustment counseling.
  - Website: https://www.vetcenter.va.gov

Continuing Your Practice

- Community: Look for local or online veteran support groups or meditation circles. Practicing with others can provide a sense of accountability and brotherhood/sisterhood.

- Apps & Tools: Many apps can help guide your daily practice. Popular and effective options include Insight Timer, Calm, and Headspace. Find one that works for you.

- Other Mind-Body Practices: Many veterans find that other practices like yoga, Tai Chi, or Qigong are powerful ways to reconnect the mind and body. Explore what is available in your community.

Deepen Your Practice: Visit our online home at www.innercoded.com to access guided meditations, workshops, and advanced articles that build upon the principles in this book.

Join the Community: Connect with a global community of fellow "decoders" who are actively applying this work in their lives. Share your insights, ask questions, and grow together.

Explore Our Frameworks: Daily Codes is the foundational practice within the InnerCoded™ ecosystem. When you are ready to take your transformation to the next level, explore our intensive programs:

- The Decode Your Day Program: A comprehensive course for systematically overhauling your mental and emotional operating system.
- The ASCEND Framework: An advanced system for aligning your life with your highest purpose.
- The Incubator Program: An immersive experience for those ready to launch their purpose into the world.

Thank you for trusting us with your journey. Continue the work.

ACKNOWLEDGMENTS

A mission like this is never accomplished alone. I am deeply grateful to the people who stood by me and made this book possible.

To my wife, Karen, you have been my rock and my partner through every phase of this journey. Your strength, love, and patience are the foundation of our family.

To my daugther, Daijah, you are my greatest teacher and my most important mission.

To the soldiers, sailors, airmen, and Marines I served alongside, and to all who have worn the uniform, the lessons we learned together are etched into every page of this book.

To my mentors and teachers in the world of mindfulness, thank you for giving me the tools to begin my own healing.

And finally, to every veteran and family member who picks up this book: thank you for your trust. May you find a piece of your own story in these pages, and may it help you find your way home.

AUTHOR PAGE:

Demetrius Irick is the founder of InnerCoded™ and the architect of a suite of transformational systems, including the ASCEND framework, the Decode Your Day Program, and The Incubator Program. A lifelong student of human behavior, his personal quest to understand the hidden patterns that shape our lives led him to his current pursuit of a Ph.D. in Behavioral Psychology.

Through his research and work, Demetrius identified a critical gap in the wellness space: an abundance of abstract concepts with a lack of practical, daily application. He founded InnerCoded™ to bridge that gap, developing a unique methodology that fuses the timeless wisdom of mindfulness with the structured logic of code. This innovative approach provides a clear and actionable system for personal evolution.

Daily Codes is the cornerstone of his philosophy, created to offer a tangible tool for transformation. His mission is to move people beyond passive self-help, empowering them to become the active architects of their own reality, one day at a time.

InnerCoded™ is a wellness collective dedicated to providing the tools for modern transformation. From the creators of the Decode Your Day Program, our work exists at the intersection of mindfulness, technology, and practical action. We believe that everyone holds the code to their own potential—they just need the right prompts to activate it.

www.ingramcontent.com/pod-product-compliance
Lightning Source LLC
Chambersburg PA
CBHW071237090426
42736CB00014B/3125